Connecting Literacy and Content

Awesome Space Robots

Level R
Science and Technology
Content: Discusses how robot technology helps people explore space.

Objectives

Students will:
- describe how robots help people explore space.
- interpret a text feature: headings and subheadings.
- monitor and clarify understanding as they read.
- do a close reading to answer questions about content.
- define and use academic vocabulary related to the text.
- use suffixes to determine meanings of words.
- read grade-level prose at an appropriate rate.
- write an informational text about a space robot.

CONNECT TO SCIENCE

Build Content Background

Engage Students

Ask: *What is a robot?* Instead of taking verbal responses, ask students to draw a picture of a robot and then have volunteers share their drawings, explaining what makes the object in the drawing a robot. Then show students a photograph of a robotic space probe or rover, such as *Curiosity*. Ask: *What is this object? What is it used for?* As students respond, guide the discussion to the questions: *Is this a robot? How is it similar and different from the robot you drew?*

Use a Graphic Organizer

Tell students that they will be reading about robots that go on space missions. Ask them to think about what they already know about robots in space exploration. Draw a KWL chart on the board or on chart paper. Explain: *We often use a KWL chart to write down what we already know about a topic, and what we want to learn about it. That helps us set a purpose for reading.* Give pairs sticky notes. Have them use sticky notes to complete the *K* column with things they already know about robots in space exploration and the *W* column with questions they have about robots, space exploration, or related topics. After reading, return to the chart so students can complete the *L* column.

Topic: Space Robots		
What I Know	What I Want to Know	What I Learned

Introduce the Content

Preview Awesome Space Robots

Give each student a copy of the text and explain: *This book is about space exploration and how robots have been used for various purposes to learn about space. Take a look at the cover. What can you learn about robots that help explore space, just by looking at the cover?* (Possible responses: They have many parts. They look complicated. They have wheels and resemble a car or tractor.) *Look through the photographs in the book. What else can you learn about robots used in space, just by looking at these photographs? What do you think you will learn from this book?* Allow a few moments for students to turn and talk to share their predictions.

Preview Academic Vocabulary

CCSS.ELA-Literacy.RI.4.4

Say: *We are reading today to answer the question: "How do robots help people explore space?" We will be coming across important vocabulary, such as* surface (p. 4), sensors (p. 6), models (p. 9), data (p. 10), atmosphere (p. 12), telescope (p. 12), *and* maintenance (p. 15), *that will help us answer this question.* Write the words on the board, and ask volunteers to identify any that seem familiar and offer sentences using them. Then read aloud a definition for each word and give additional explanations or examples to clarify the meaning of each one. Finally, point out the bold words throughout the text and tell students that the glossary on p. 30 defines these words.

Awesome Space Robots

9781620657799

Discuss Text Features
CCSS.ELA-Literacy.RI.4.5

Say: *Authors of informational texts often use headings and subheadings to divide the text into sections. The main headings in this book are chapter titles, which can also be seen in the table of contents on page 3. The chapter titles break the text into large sections. Subheadings within each chapter divide it into smaller sections.* Point out the chapter title on p. 8: *Building a Robotic Explorer.* Explain that the whole chapter will relate to the chapter title, so readers can expect to learn about the process of building a robotic explorer. Ask: *What are the subheadings in this chapter? What do you think each section will be about? How does each one support the main topic of the chapter?* Have pairs turn and talk before answering the questions.

Focus on the Content

As you focus on the text, ask questions that require students to use varying depths of knowledge. Model how to determine the answer to a question before you pose additional questions. (A model is shown for the first question.)

- **Compare** (pp. 6–7) *How are space robots similar to other robots? How are they different?* (Possible response: Space robots have sensors to detect what is around them, and computers to guide their responses, similar to other robots. They also have tools to do their tasks and a power source to give them power. However, they are specially designed to do tasks in space, such as fly past a planet or other object, orbit a planet or moon, or land on a planet or moon to explore.)

Model *This question is asking me to compare space robots with other robots. As I look at page 6, I read the words* "Like all robots," *This is a clue that the author is going to tell me how space robots are like other robots.*

Collaborate *Partners, read page 6 together. Read to identify ways that space robots are like other robots.*

Provide Independent Practice Have students read on to find ways that space robots are different from other robots. Tell them to focus on the jobs that the robots do to find the main differences.

Summarize *We've listed the similarities space robots share with all robots, and the ways that space robots are different. We learned that space robots have very unique jobs.*

- **Identify** (p. 8) *What do scientists do before they start designing a new space robot?* (They think of a question they want to be able to answer using the robot.)
- **Infer** (p. 9) *What conditions during a mission are most likely to cause damage to a space robot?* (violent shaking during launch and landing, extreme cold, and extreme heat)
- **Explain** (pp. 14–15) *How do robots help astronauts on the International Space Station?* (Possible response: The Canadarm is a robotic arm that helps astronauts on the International Space Station lift and move heavy things, and do maintenance work on the station. The Robonaut 2 helps astronauts test airflow in the station's air vents, but could also be used for other tasks in the future.)
- **Classify** (pp. 16–22) *Which space robots have explored the solar system's giant gas planets? Which planet or planets did each study?* (*Voyager 1* explored Jupiter and Saturn. *Voyager 2* explored Jupiter, Saturn, Uranus, and Neptune. *Galileo* and *Juno* explored Jupiter and its moons. *Cassini* studied Saturn and its moons.)
- **Compare** (pp. 26–27) *How were the missions of* Spirit *and* Opportunity *similar to the mission of* Curiosity? (Possible responses: They all explored the surface of Mars. They all tested samples of material on Mars's surface.)

Discuss Concepts

Ask:

- *What are the four types of space robots, and what does each one do?* (Probes are sent on simple missions. They fly past planets, moons, and other objects in space to take photographs and measurements. Orbiters stay in orbit around a planet or moon for a long time to study changes in its atmosphere or surface. Landers stay in one spot on a planet and study just that part of its surface. Rovers drive around a planet or moon and explore a large area of the surface.)
- *What tasks do space robots perform that help us learn about space?* (Answers will vary. Possible responses: They take photographs that show us what different planets, moons, and other objects look like. They test soil and rock on other planets and moons to learn more about what substances make up these objects. They collect information about atmospheres of other planets.)
- *Why do you think we have sent so many robots to Mars?* (Answers will vary. Possible responses: Mars is close to us, and people think we might send astronauts there one day. People have been curious about Mars for a long time because it can be seen from Earth.)

Apply Concepts Have students return to the KWL chart they began at the beginning of the book. Have them add details to the *L* column of the chart using sticky notes. They might add facts they learned from the reading and new ideas they had while discussing the book with partners or with the class. Have volunteers share what they are adding to the chart.

Clarifying/Monitoring

CCSS.ELA-Literacy.RI.4.3

Introduce the Strategy Say: *Sometimes when we read, we come across words or ideas that we don't understand. If something doesn't make sense, what can we do? We can slow down or pause, we can ask ourselves questions about what we're reading, we can reread the text, or we can figure out what new words mean. All of these strategies can help us understand the text and its ideas.*

Model Focus on p. 24. Say: *Listen as I read the text aloud.* Stop at the word *equipped.* Say: *I am not sure what this word means. But I see some clues. The word* equip *looks like it is related to the word* equipment, *which I know means the tools you need to do a task. I read that the landers* "were equipped with cameras and robotic ... arms." *This makes it sound like* equipped *means that the landers came with these tools. Does that make sense? Yes, this makes sense in the text.*

Guide Practice Have students work with a partner and reread a section of text they find difficult, monitoring their reading using one of the strategies above. Encourage students to turn and talk with a partner about which part they found confusing and what they did to better understand it.

Close Reading

CCSS.ELA-Literacy.RI.4.1, RI.4.2

Introduce the Strategy Say: *When we answer a question about the text, we should not rely only on our own knowledge or what we think about the topic. To make sure we are basing our answers on the text, we need to reread it closely. That means we go back to the author's words on the page to find evidence to support our answers.*

Model Project pp. 26–27 on the whiteboard or a piece of chart paper, and model how to find text evidence to answer the second **Compare** question: *This question asks me tell how the missions of* Spirit *and* Opportunity *were similar to the mission of* Curiosity. *I'll start reading on page 26 under the heading* Spirit *and* Opportunity *Arrive to find text evidence for my answer. I read that* Spirit *and* Opportunity *were set to explore* "the harsh terrain" *of Mars and that they studied ground-up rocks to discover the minerals and salts in them. I am marking these ideas with a highlighter to remember them. Turning to page 27, I read about* Curiosity. *I'll highlight* "landed on Mars" *and* "zap rocks and study their makeup." Model highlighting the text on the whiteboard or chart paper.

Guide Practice Provide copies of pp. 14–15 along with highlighters. Have students highlight textual evidence on the copies to answer the **Explain** question.

Focus on Fluency

CCSS.ELA-Literacy.RF.4.4b

Model Fluent Reading Say: *Fluent readers try to read at a rate, or speed, that makes a text understandable and easy to follow. It is important to read at a rate that isn't too fast or too slow. You can also speed up in some places and slow down in others, to match what is happening in the text. Listen carefully as I read the text on page 21.* Read the text quickly, without pausing at the punctuation. Point out that this is hard to follow and understand. Read the same section again, but too slowly. Point out that it is easy to lose track of the meaning of the text when you read it too slowly. Finally, read the text fluently at a reasonable rate, pausing at the punctuation.

Guide Practice Choose another passage from the book for students to practice reading at an appropriate rate. Have students pair up and read the passage to each other. Circulate and offer assistance as needed.

Study Words

CCSS.ELA-Literacy.L.4.4b

Introduce the Strategy Say: *Affixes are word parts that we add to base words to change their meanings. A suffix is an affix that is added to the end of a word. For example, we know that by adding the suffix* –ness *to a word, we change its meaning to* state of being: *happy, happiness.*

Practice the Strategy Focus on the words *useless* (p. 10) and *valuable* (p. 16) in the text. Write the words on the board or chart paper. Have students separate the suffix from the base word in each (*use/less; value/able*). Discuss the meanings of these suffixes. Say: *The suffix* –less *means* without *and the suffix* –able *means* has the ability to be. *How do the suffixes change the meanings of the base words? What other words can you name with these suffixes?*

Discuss the Text

CCSS.ELA-Literacy.RI.4.1, RI.4.3

Have students focus on these questions about the text:

- **Analyze** *Look at this sentence on page 10:* "The large 'wings' on many space probes are made of solar cells." *Why did the author place the word* wings *in quotation marks? What does this sentence tell you about space probes?* (Possible response: The author is saying that the large panels of solar cells, like those shown on p. 13, look like the wings of an airplane or bird. Since the solar cells don't actually help the space probe fly, the author uses the quotation marks.)
- **Draw Conclusions** *The author says that the* Voyager *mission was the* "most important deep space mission [NASA] had ever attempted." *Why do you think the* Voyagers *are considered so important?* (Answers will vary. Students may suggest that *Voyager 1* and *Voyager 2* were the first space probes to be sent to other planets or that they continue to send important information from very far away.)
- **Design** *To design a new robot, scientists think of a question they want it to answer. What question would you like to answer about space? What features would a robot need to answer this question?* (Answers will vary. Accept all reasonable responses.)

Provide Prompts for Response

Offer prompts that allow students to explore the text:

- Draw a four-column chart to classify each robot in the book as a probe, lander, rover, or orbiter.
- Use three vocabulary terms from the text in sentences about space robots.
- Tell which ideas were new to you. What questions do you still have about space robots?
- Which parts of the book were easiest to understand? Which were the most difficult?

Connect with Writing: Informational Text

CCSS.ELA-Literacy.W.4.2a, W.4.2b, W.4.2c, W.4.2d

Introduce the Text Type and Assignment Say: *Authors of informational texts provide facts, descriptions, and examples to help readers understand a topic. This book includes an overview of many different missions to space that involved robots, but I'm curious to find out more information about these missions. I'd like to know what scientists discovered, and I'd enjoy seeing some of the photographs taken by the robots as they explored space. So, today you are going to choose a mission that is discussed in the text, research that mission, and write an informational text based on your research.*

Review Features Review the features of an informational text, and be sure to display these features for students' reference:

- An introduction that focuses readers on the topic
- Interesting facts and details
- Content-specific vocabulary
- Text features, such as subheadings, photographs, and diagrams
- A strong conclusion that summarizes main ideas and provides closure

Model the Writing Model the writing process as you begin a text that that details the *Cassini-Huygens* mission: *I decided to write about the* Cassini-Huygens *mission. Watch as I begin my model with a description of the purpose of the mission:*

In 1997, NASA worked together with the European Space Agency and the Italian space agency, Agenzia Spaziale Italiana, to send a robotic explorer to Saturn. Scientists wanted to investigate Saturn over a long period of time, taking photographs of its surface and atmosphere. They designed *Cassini*—an orbiter that would orbit the planet and collect data about its surface, atmosphere, and rings. Scientists also wanted to investigate the surface of Saturn's moons, so they designed *Huygens*—a lander.

Notice that I started by introducing the topic and giving a description of some of the complex work this mission was designed for. Model one more section of the text, explaining how *Cassini* established an orbit around Saturn in 2004 and *Huygens* landed on Saturn's moon Titan in 2005.

Support Writers Display your model as students begin writing. Remind them that their writing should include facts, definitions, specific details, examples, and content-specific vocabulary. Support students as they add text features to their writing, such as subheadings, diagrams, photographs, and captions.

Revise and Edit Show students how to revise and edit for specific points, such as:

- Logical organization
- Sentence variety
- Transitions
- Correct grammar, capitalization, and spelling

Share and Reflect Allow time for students to share their work with an authentic audience. Then ask questions to guide self-reflection:

- What is the most fascinating thing you learned from your research?
- What did you want readers to learn about the robot you chose? Do you think you accomplished your goal?
- What did you learn about the writing process that will help when you write your next paper?